CNA EXAM PREP

Nurse Assistant Practice Test Questions

Jane John-Nwankwo RN, MSN

CNA EXAM PREP: Nurse Assistant Practice Test Questions

ISBN-13: 978-1482355475

ISBN-10: 1482355477

Printed in USA by Createspace Publishing.

Dedication

Dedicated to my husband, John Nwankwo who gave me all the support to publish this book

TABLE OF CONTENTS

Section One……………………………………..……..5

Section Two ………………………….……………...34

Section Three……………………………………….63

SECTION ONE

1. A state of being unaware of one's surroundings and being unable to react or respond to people, places or things is called:

   A. Shock
   B. Coma
   C. Fainting
   D. Sleeping

2. Paralysis on one side of the body is____________.

   A. Quadriplegia
   B. Paraplegia
   C. Hemiplegia
   D. Lame

3. These are safety measures for infants and children except:

   A. Check infants often when in cribs.
   B. Always use pin on children's clothing
   C. Unplug electrical items when not in use
   D. Install safety guards on windows

4. A resident's ID bracelet contains the following information except:

   A. The resident's driver's license
   B. The name
   C. The Room and Bed number

D. Know allergies

5. Most falls occur in the evening, between_____.

A. 3:00pm and 9:00pm
B. 4:00pm and 5:00pm
C. 5:00pm and 6:00pm
D. 1800 and 2100

6. People in greatest risk of bed rail entrapment are the following except:

A. Hypertensive residents
B. Confused and disoriented residents
C. Are small in size
D. Are restrained.

7. These are not one of the safety alerts in bed rails:

A. If the person uses bed rails, always raise the far bed rail if you are working alone.
B. Never leave the person alone when the bed is raised
C. Raise both bed rails if you need to leave the bedside for any reason
D. If the person does not use bed rail, go ahead and raise it since is for the resident's good.

8. Safety measures to prevent burns in children are the following except:

A. Do not leave children home alone
B. Supervise young children at all times
C. Encourage children to help you cook
D. Cover car seats with towels if you park in the sun.

9. One of the following is a prevention of poisoning in children:

A. Be sure people smoke only in smoking areas
B. Keep childproof caps on all harmful substances
C. Do not use electric blankets
D. Do not leave children unattended in bath.

10. All these are characteristics of the poisonous carbon monoxide except:

A. Is Tasteless
B. Is colorful
C. It is produced by the burning of fuel
D. Is colorless

11. The following should be done to an agitated and aggressive person except.

A. Shouting to person when talking
B. Stand away from the person
C. Talk to the person without raising your voice
D. Stand close to the door

12. Which of the following is unsafe when a resident is using a wheelchair?

A. Brakes are locked for transfers
B. The brakes are locked when he is resting.
C. The casters point forward
D. The resident can stand on the footplates

13. When electrical current passes through the body it becomes______

A. Electrical surge
B. Electrical coma
C. Electrical shock
D. Grounding

14. Warnings of faulty electrical items include the followings except:

A. Tight plugs
B. Shocks
C. Burning odor
D. Sizzling or buzzing sounds

15. A_________ substance is any chemical in the work place that can cause harm.

A. Safe
B. Liquid
C. Hazardous
D. None of the above

16. RACE is what to during a ________

A. During Residents riot
B. During a fire incident
C. During employees strike
D. During heated arguments

17. These are safety measures where oxygen is used except:

A. No smoking signs are placed on the door and near the bed
B. Smoking materials, matches, and lighters are removed from the room
C. Electrical items are left on before been turned off
D. The person and visitors are reminded no to smoke in the room

18. A Sudden catastrophic event is called_______.

A. Confusion
B. Misunderstanding
C. Quarrel
D. Disaster

19. One of the measures that can prevent or control work place violence is:

A. Do not touch the person
B. Stand close to the person
C. Speak to the person in an aggressive manner
D. Stand away from the door

20. Risk management deals with these issues except :

A. Accident and fire prevention
B. State and county requirements
C. Patient and resident abuse
D. Negligence and malpractice

21. The followings are risk of accidents except:

A. Alertness
B. Poor Vision
C. Memory lapses
D. Hearing impairment

22. The following can cause fire out break except:

A. CO
B. O_2
C. A spark or flame
D. A material with burning ability

23. What is the meaning of R in RACE during fire outbreak?

A. Run away
B. Retreat
C. Rescue
D. Remain there

24. During evacuation which people are taken out first?

A. Elder people
B. Female residents
C. Younger people
D. People closest to danger of fire

25. These are fire prevention measures except:

A. Smoke only where allowed to do so
B. Allow children to play freely
C. Supervise persons who smoke
D. Follow safety measures for oxygen use

Circle T if the statement is true and F if it is false

26. T F Drugs used in cancer therapy are hazardous substances.
27. T F Health hazards can cause cancer.
28. T F Loose plugs can be a sign of faulty electrical item.
29. T F Run electrical cords under rug for safety.
30. T F Wheelchairs and stretchers wheels are locked during transfers.
31. T F Hand rails give support to people who are weak or unsteady when walking.
32. T F Supervise children at all in time aids in preventing burns.
33. T F Rearranging furniture is a safety measure in preventing falls.
34. T F The risk of falling increases with age.
35. T F People older than 65 years are at high risk of falling.
36. T F Paraplegia is the paralysis from the waist down.

37. T F Quadriplegia is paralysis on one side.
38. T F Suffocation is when breathing stops from the lack of oxygen.
39. T F Safety measures in infants includes allowing them to ride in front seat of cars.
40. T F Ground is that which carries leaking electricity to the earth and away from an electrical item.
41. T F History of falls are one of the factors increasing the risk of fall.
42. T F providing safety rails and grab bars in showers are one of the measures to prevent falls.

43 The study of the aging process is called______.

A. Geriatrics
B. Gerontology
C. Anatomy
D. Physiology

44. The usual retirement age is_____ years.

A. 45
B. 87
C. 65
D. 55

45. The following are physical reminders of growing old except:

A. Fast Movements
B. Graying hair
C. Wrinkles
D. Slow Movements

46. Young-old people are between ______ years.

A. 65 and 80
B. 75 and 84
C. 85

D. 65 and 74

47. Someone who supports or promotes the needs and interests of another person is called;

A. Negotiator
B. Solicitor
C. Ombudsman
D. Intermediary

48. The care of aging people is ________.

A. Pediatrics
B. Geriatrics
C. Gynecology
D. Gerontology

49. Brown spots that appear on the skin of older people are called:

A. Kidney spots
B. Heart spots
C. Rectal spots
D. Liver spots

50. The followings are rights of the residents except:

A. The person is required to perform services for the center
B. The person has the right to be fully informed of his or her total health condition.
C. Residents have right to use the bathroom in privacy
D. Residents can choose their own doctors

51. When a resident refuse treatment the CNA should_______

A. Threatened the resident about the treatment
B. Go ahead with the treatment since is for the resident good.
C. Report any treatment refusal to the charge nurse
D. Call the resident family immediately telling them what happened

52. Retirement usually accompanies with______.

A. Higher income earning
B. Reduced income
C. Financial Security
D. Aging

53. Aging causes changes in the nervous system. Which is false?

A. Fewer nerve cells
B. Reflexes becomes slow
C. Sleep patterns changes
D. Skin becomes less elastic.

54. These are changes in the digestive system of aging people except:

A. Decreased saliva production
B. Heart pumps with less force
C. Difficulty in swallowing
D. Loss of teeth

55. In integumentary system of aging people which one of the followings usually happen?

A. Skin thins and sags
B. Bone mass decreases
C. Arteries narrow and are less elastic
D. Urinary urgency may occur

56. Which of the followings are not noticed when an aging person loses the partner:

A. Grief may be great
B. Serious physical and mental health problem may arise
C. They normally live happier
D. Some attempt suicide

57. These changes occur in the musculoskeletal aging people except:

A. Bladder muscles weaken
B. Muscle atrophy
C. Bone strength decreases
D. Bones become brittle.

58. Helping aging people with poor eyesight involves the following except:

A. Increase light bulb
B. Lights in closet and hallways
C. Increase phone volume
D. Phone with a large keypad

59. Which of the following is not a feature of a good nursing center?

A. Hallways are wide enough for 2 wheelchairs to pass with ease
B. Resident rooms have no windows
C. Resident rooms open to the hallway
D. The center is Medicare and Medicaid certified.

60. OBRA environment requirements are these except:

A. There are no glares

B. The person's needs are met
C. Halls have handrails
D. Tables are of very low height

61. The physical changes that are measured and occur in a steady, orderly manner is called?

A. Development
B. A stage
C. Growth
D. A reflex

62. The first menstruation and start of menstrual cycle is_______.

A. Puberty
B. Ovulation
C. Menopause
D. Menarche

63. The following are principles of growth and development except:

A. The process at fertilization and continues until death.
B. The process proceeds from the simple to complex.
C. The rate of process is even and it is at a set pace.
D. The process occurs in a sequence, order and pattern.

64. The first year of life is?

A. Adulthood
B. Infancy
C. Adolescence
D. Puberty

65. An infant can walk while holding onto something at about____.

A. 10months
B. 6 months
C. 4 months
D 2 months

66. The developmental tasks of infancy are:

A. Learning to walk
B. Learning to eat solid foods
C. Beginning to talk and communicate with others.
D. All of the above

67. The neonatal period of infancy is from birth to______.

A. 3 months
B. 1 month
C. 5 months
D. 9 months

68. The time between puberty and adulthood is

A. Childhood
B. Infancy
C. Adolescence
D. Youth

69. The period when reproductive organs begin to function and the secondary sex characteristics appears is ____>

A. Adolescence
B. Puberty
C. Menopause
D. Growth

70. Girls reach puberty between the ages of ____ years.

A. 9 and 15

B. 9 and 18
C. 12 and 16
D. 12 and 18

71. The developmental tasks of adolescence include all except:

A. Accepting changes in the body and appearance
B. Developing appropriate relationships with males and females of the same age
C. Becoming a parent and raising children.
D. developing morals, attitude and values needed to function in the society.

72. Which is not a developmental task of young adulthood?

A. Adjusting to physical changes
B. Selecting a partner
C. Learning to live with a partner
D. Developing a satisfactory sex life

73. Young adulthood is from about _____years.

A. 12 to 18
B. 18 to 40
C. 40 to 65
D. 65

74. Boys usually stop growing between the ages of:

A. 18 to 4o years
B. 10 to 15 years
C. 18 to 21 years
D. 17 to 18 years

75. The reflex observed when a baby is startled by a loud noise, a sudden movement, or the head falling back is _____

A. Rooting reflex
B. Sucking reflex
C. Grasp reflex
D. Moro reflex

76. A skill that must be completed during a stage development is:

A. Principles
B. Developmental task
C. Developmental process
D. Stage development

77. Which statement is false?

A. Menarche marks the onset of puberty in girls
B. Girls reach puberty between the ages of 9 and 15 years
C. Adolescence is a time of rapid growth, physical and social maturity
D. Boys reach puberty earlier than girls.

78. Middle adulthood is a time when;

A. Children are grown-up and leave home
B. Coping with a partner's death
C. Families are started
D. Physical energy increases

79. Process in which the lining of the uterus breaks up and is discharged from the body through the vagina is:

A. Menstruation
B. Circulation

C. Metabolism
D. Digestion

80. A situation where a person has protection against a certain disease or condition is called:

A. Germicide
B. Immunity
C. Vaccine
D. Personal protective equipment

81. The basic unit of body structure is_____.

A. Organs
B. Tissue
C. Hormone
D. Cells

82. Which is not an example of organs?

A. Liver
B. Lungs
C. Cell
D. Nose

83. The substance in red blood cells that carries oxygen and gives blood its color is ______.

A. Hormone
B. Hemoglobin
C. Platelets
D. Organs

84. A blood vessel that carries blood away from the heart is:

A. Vein
B. Valve

C. Capillary
D. Artery

85. The largest artery that receives blood directly from the left ventricle is ______.

A. Aorta
B. Veins
C. Pericardium
D. Arteriole

86. Which is not a function of the skin?

A. It helps regulates body temperature
B. It provide framework for the body
C. It protects organs from injury
D. It prevents bacteria and other substances from entering the body.

87. Human body has how many bones?

A. 205 bones
B. 200 bones
C. 206 bones
D. 360 bones

88. Which statement about bones is false?

A. Bones carries blood to the chest.
B. They are rigid structures.
C. They are made up of living cells.
D. Bones are covered by a membrane called periosteum

89. Which is not a function of muscle?

A. Movement of body parts
B. Protection of organs

C. Maintenance of posture
D. Production of body heat.

90. The largest part of the brain which is the center of thought and intelligence is?

A. Brainstem
B. Cerebellum
C. Cerebrum
D. Skull.

91. Which parts of the brain regulates and coordinates body movement and also controls balance and smooth movement of the voluntary, muscles?

A. Medulla
B. Brainstem
C. Cerebrum
D. Cerebellum

92. The brain and the spinal cord are covered and protected by three layers of connective tissues called?

A. Arachnoid
B. Pia mater
C. Dura Mater
D. Meninges

93. The Receptors for smell are in ____.

A. Eyes
B. Dermis
C. Nose
D. Tongue

94. Red blood cells are called______.

A. Erythrocytes

B. Leukocytes
C. Platelets
D. Thrombocytes.

95. The process of supplying the cell with oxygen and removing carbon dioxide from them is:

A. Circulation
B. Respiration
C. Reproduction
D. Digestion

96. Involuntary muscle contractions in digestive system that moves food through the alimentary canal is_____.

A. Intestine
B. Rectum
C. Chyme
D. Peristalsis

97. Which part of the heart receives blood from the body tissues?

A. The Right Atrium
B. The Left atrium
C. Right Ventricle
D. Left ventricle

98. The Fusion of the sperm and ovum into one cell is called:

A. Ovulation
B. Reproduction
C. Fertilization
D. Menstruation

99. The external vaginal Opening is partially closed by a membrane called:

A. Clitoris
B. Hymen
C. Urethra
D. Mons Pubis

100. The use of body language when communicating to another person is part of which type of communication?

A. Verbal communication.
B. Non-verbal communication.
C. Electronic communication.
D. Written communication.

101.When clients express their feelings and concerns,the CNA should respond by:

A. Asking question.
B. Giving clients suggestions.
C Listening to the clients concerns.
D. Sharing his/her family problems.

102. Listening requires that you care and have interest, which is not guidelines for good listening:

A. Sitting back with your arms crossed.
B. Facing the person.
C. Lean towards the person.
D. Having good eye contact with the person.

103. Lack of eye contact can mean the following Except:

A. Shyness.
B. High self-esteem.
C. Lack of interest.
D. Guilt.

104. Restating the person's message in your own words is:

A. Paraphrasing.
B. Clarifying.
C. Listening.
D. Focusing.

105. Paraphrasing shows that:

A. You are listening.
B. Lets the person see if you understand the message sent.
C. Promote further communication.
D. All of the above.

106. Which one is not an example of open-ended questions?

A. "What do you like about living with your daughter."
B. "Tell me about your grandson."
C. "Do you want to shave this morning."
D. "What do you like about being retired?"

107. Questions that lead or invite the person to share thoughts, feelings, or ideas is:

A. Direct question.
B. Indirect question.
C. Questions.
D. Open-ended question.

108. Miss. Stone is comatose, which action is false?

A. Explain what you are going to do.
B. Use silence to communicate.
C. Assume that she can hear you.
D. Tell her when you are living the room.

109. As a CNA, when dealing with behavior issues you should do the followings
Except:

A. Recognize frustrating and frightening situations.
B. Not argue with the person.
C. Protect yourself from violent behavior.
D. Hit the person hard.

110. When communicating with foreign speaking persons you should do the followings Except:

A. Speak loudly.
B. Convey comfort by your tone of voice and body language.
C. Keep message short and simple.
D. Use gestures and pictures.

111. Which of the followings is not physiological need?

A. Water.
B. Food.
C. Friendship.
D. Oxygen.

112. Which basic needs is most essential?

A. Physiological needs.
B. Love and belonging needs.
C. Self-esteem needs.
D. Safety and security needs.

113. Which statement is False about silence?

A. Silence shows disrespect for the person's situation and feelings
B. Silence gives time to think, organize thoughts, or choose words.
C. It helps when the person is upset and needs to regain

control.

D. Silence is useful when making decisions.

114. Focusing is useful when:

A. You want to understand the message.
B. A person rambles or wanders in thought.
C. You want the person to share his feelings.
D. Want to get certain information.

115. Branch of medicine concerned with the problems and disease of old age and older persons is:

A. Holism.
B. Pediatrics.
C. Geriatrics.
D. Psychiatry.

116. Which is not barriers for effective communication?

A. Cultural difference.
B. Changing the subject.
C. Talking a lot when others are silent.
D. Using familiar language.

117. A lost, absent, or impaired physical or mental function is?

A. Disability.
B. Fear.
C. Esteem.
D. Malfunction.

118. Mr. Jackson was moved out of his home and into a

long-term care facility, He
is angry about being moved. The CNA should:

A. Ignore the behavior.
B. Sit with him and talk about his feelings.
C. Ask another staff member to care for him.
D. Tell him that he will get used to the facility.

119. A visitor seems to upset or tire a person, you should:

A. Report your observation to the nurse.
B. Ask the visitor to leave.
C. Stay in the room.
D. Slap the visitor.

120. Using Maslow's theory of basic needs, which person's need must be met first?

A. Mr. Jackson, who is crying.
B. Mr. Wood, who wants his mail opened.
C. Mr. Johnson, who asks for more water.
D. Mr. Ben, who wants another blankets.

121. Information that you can see, hear, feel or smell is called?

A. Subjective data.
B. Observation.
C. Evaluation.
D. Objective data.

122. The identification of a disease or condition by a doctor is:

A. Nursing diagnosis.
B. Medical diagnosis.

C. Nursing intervention.
D. Medical intervention.

123. Which of the following is not step in nursing process?

A. Communication.
B. Planning.
C. Implementation.
D. Evaluation.

124. Things a person tells you about that you cannot observe through your senses is:

A. Objective data.
B. Goal.
C. Subjective data.
D. Implementation.

125. Which statement is not true about a goal?

A. A goal is that which is desired in or by a person as a result of nursing care.
B. Goals are not set.
C. Goals promote health and prevent health problems.
D. Goals promote rehabilitation.

126. The assignment sheet tell you about:

A. Each person's care.
B. What measures and tasks need to be done.
C. Which nursing tasks to do.
D. All of the above.

127. Reporting what a clients tell you is :

A. Subjective observation.
B. Objective observation.
C. Primary observation.
D. Secondary observation.

128. Measures taken by the nursing team to help the person reach a goal is called?

A. Nursing care plan.
B. Nursing intervention.
C. Nursing process.
D. Nursing diagnosis.

129. What happens during planning?

A. Goals are set.
B. Progress is evaluated.
C. Tasks are performed.
D. Information is collected.

130. Which of these is not medical diagnosis?

A. Chickenpox.
B. Pain.
C. AIDS.
D. Pneumonia.

ANSWERS TO SECTION ONE

1. B
2. C
3. B
4. A
5. D
6. A
7. D
8. C
9. B
10. B
11. A
12. D
13. C
14. A
15. C
16. B
17. C
18. D
19. A
20. B
21. A
22. A
23. C
24. D
25. B
26. T
27. T
28. T
29. F
30. T
31. T
32. T
33. T
34. T

35. T
36. T
37. F
38. T
39. F
40. T
41. T
42. T
43. B
44. C
45. A
46. D
47. C
48. B
49. D
50. A
51. C
52. B
53. D
54. B
55. A
56. C
57. A
58. C
59. B
60. D
61. C
62. D
63. C
64. B
65. A
66. D
67. B
68. C
69. B
70. A
71. C

72. A
73. B
74. C
75. D
76. B
77. D
78. A
79. A
80. B
81. D
82. C
83. B
84. D
85. A
86. B
87. C
88. A
89. B
90. C
91. D
92. D
93. C
94. A
95. B
96. D
97. A
98. C
99. B
100.B.
101.C.
102.A.
103.B.
104.A.
105.D.
106.C.
107.D.
108.B.
109.D.

110.A.
111.C.
112.D.
113.A.
114.B.
115.C.
116.D.
117.A.
118.B.
119.A.
120.C.
121.D.
122.B.
123.A.
124.C.
125.B.
126.D.
127.A.
128.B.
129.A.
130.B.

SECTION TWO

1. Which of these is not a guideline for completing a job application?

A. Read and follow the directions.

B. Lying on an application.

C. Write neatly.

D. Give information about employment gap.

2. Courtesy is?

A. Behavior in the work place.

B. Seeing things from other person's point of view.

C. Polite or helpful comment or act.

D. Feeling sorry for a person.

3. Work ethics involves the following except:

A. How others walk.

B. How you look.

C. What you say.

D. How you behave.

4. Good work ethics involves these qualities and traits except:

A. Gossiping.

B. Dependable.

C. Courteous.

D. Trustworthy.

5. The response or change in the body caused by any emotional, physical, social or

Economic factor is:

A. Sleep.

B. Weight.

C. Drugs.

D. Stress.

6. Stress can be reduced by one of the followings:

A. Planning personal and quite time.

B. Shouting and screaming.

C. Judging yourself harshly.
D. Blaming yourself for thing you did not do.

7. The best response to an interview question is:
A. Long answers.
B. Short answers.
C. "Yes" or "No".
D. Brief explanation.

8. All is a common interview questions except:
A. Tell me about yourself.
B. Tell me about your career goals.
C. Where do you study?
D. How do you set priorities?

9. Which of these is not a good behavior during a job interview?
A. Sitting in a professional manner.
B. Touching or reading things on the interviewer's desk.
C. Good eye contact with an interviewer.
D. Maintaining good body language.

10. One of these is NOT professional speech and language:
A. Speaking softly and gently.
B. Speaking clearly.
C. Cursing and yelling.
D. Good relationship with the person and family.

11. Good hygiene for work involves the followings:
A. Bathing daily.
B. Using a deodorant or antiperspirant.
C. Keeping fingernails clean, short and neatly shaped.
D. All of the above.

12. Practices for a professional appearance involves the followings except:
A. Practice good hygiene.
B. Wear uniform that fit well.
C. Wear jewelry in pierced eyebrows and nose.

D. Wear your name badge or photo ID at all times when on duty.

13. How should a nurse aid dress for a job interview?
A .Wearing a clean t-shirt and casual slacks.
B. Wearing a business suit, dress, or pants and shirt.
C. Wearing formal attire.
D. Wearing nurse aid uniform.

14. All employers want employees who are:
A. Dependable.
B. Well-groomed.
C. Have the needed job skills and training.
D. All of the above.

15. Guidelines for job safety practices include the followings except:
A. Understanding the roles, functions and responsibilities in your job
Description.
B. Know the contents and policies in personnel and procedure manuals.
C. Gossiping with co-workers.
D. Know what you can and cannot do.

16. These statements are about gossip. Which one is false?
A. Gossip spread rumors.
B. Gossip is hurtful.
C. Gossip is to talk about the private matters of others.
D. Gossip is professional and not hurtful.

17. A co-worker tells you that a nurse and patient are dating. This is?
A. Confidential information.
B. Gossip.
C. Sexual harassment.
D. Eavesdropping.

18. Keeping personal matters out of the work place includes the followings except

A. Making personal phone calls only during meals and breaks.

B. Controlling your emotions.

C. Discussing personal problems at work.

D. Turn off personal pagers or wireless phone while at work.

19. When planning your work you should do the following except:

A. Discuss priorities with the nurse.

B. Know the routine of your shift and nursing unit.

C. Leave a messy work area.

D. Judge how much time you need for each person, procedure and task.

20. To trouble, torment, offend or worry a person by one's behavior or comment
is called?

A. Stress.

B. Harassment.

C. Courtesy.

D. Gossip.

21. These statements signal a bad attitude except:

A. "Please show me how this works."

B. " I work harder than anyone else."

C. "No one appreciates what I do."

D. I can't. I'm too busy."

22. Which one is not a common reason for losing a job?

A. Using offensive speech and language.

B. Stealing the agency's or person's property.

C. Having weapons in the work setting.

D. Having good values and attitudes that fit the agency.

23. The best definition of certified nursing assistant is a:

A. Person who transcribes the doctor's order for patient care.

B. Licensed person who provides education about

special diets.
C. Person who is certified to give care under the direct supervision
D. Graduate nurse who is registered and licensed by the
of a registered or licensed practical nurse
the state to practice nursing.

24. A nurse who has completed a 2-,3-, or 4-year nursing program
and has passed a licensed test is:

A. Licensed vocational nurse.
B. Registered nurse.
C. Physician.
D. CNA

25. Which of the following is not a member of long-term healthcare team?

A. Charge nurse.
B. Nursing supervisor.
C. Receptionist.
D. Nursing assistant.

26. As a CNA,your important role in meeting standards and survey process
includes:

A. Providing quality care.
B. Protecting the person's rights.
C. Conducting yourself in a professional manner.
D. All of the above.

27. The purpose of long-term care facility is:

A. To provide emergency care for blind people.
B. To provide care for persons who cannot care for themselves at home.
C. To provide surgical care for mental people
D. None of the above.

28. A sudden illness from which a person is expected to recover is?

A. Chronic illness.
B. Terminal illness.
C. Acute illness.
D. Hospice.

29. The goal of rehabilitation and restorative care is to:

A .Return persons to their highest possible level of physical and psychological functioning.
B. Worsen resident condition.
C. Do surgery.
D. Provide clients with privacy.

30. All long-term care nurse aids must be competency and evaluated and must complete a distinct educational course,these requirement are set by:

A. OBRA
B. HIPAA
C. OSHA
D. CDC.

31. Who assists person to learn or retain skills and designs adaptive equipment needed to perform activities of daily living?

A. Nursing assistant.
B. Medical technologist(MT).
C. Dietitian.
D. Occupational therapist(OT).

32. Responsibilities of a CNA are listed in a:

A. Job title.
B. Job description.
C. Job credentials.
D. Procedure.

33. The purpose of health care is to:

A. Promote good health.
B. Prevent disease.
C. Detect and treat disease.
D. All of the above

34. A healthcare payment program sponsored by federal & state government is:

A. Medicaid.
B. Healthcare.
C. Insurance.
D. Team care.

35. Any item, object, device, garment, material or drug that limits or restricts person's freedom of movement or access to one's body is ________.

A. Protector.
B. Safety guide
C. A restraint
D. Device

36. Restraints are for the following people except:

A. Confused person
B. Blind people
C. Person with behavior problem
D. People who has poor judgment

37. Which is not risk of restraints use?

A. Shock
B. Depression
C. Bruises
D. Fractures

38. Discipline is any action that:

A. Controls the person's behavior
B. Requires less effort by the agency
C. Is not in the person's best interest
D. That punishes or penalizes a person

39. According to OBRA and CMS, physical restraints includes these except:

A. Is attached to or next to the person's body
B. Controls mental function
C. Restricts freedom of movement or access to one's body
D. Cannot be easily removed by the person

40. Physical restraints are applied to the following places except:

A. Chest
B. Waist
C. Eyes
D. Wrists

41. These are risks of restraint use except:

A. Agitation
B. Dehydration
C. Cuts
D. Trust

42. Information about restraints is recorded in the person's __________.

A. Nursing history
B. Medical record
C. Intake and output chart
D. Graph sheet

43. Leather restraints are applied to_______.

A. Wrists and ankles
B. Eyes and head
C. Mouth and nose
D. Mouth and fingers

44. When charting you should include the following information:

A. The type of restraint applied
B. The body part or parts restrained
C. The reason for the application
D. All of the above

45. Writs restraints limit_______ movements.

A. Hip
B. Leg
C. Arm
D. Finger

46. The straps of vest and jacket restraints always cross in:

A. Centre
B. Side
C. Front
D. Back

47. The safety belt is always in__________ angle.

A. 45
B. 100
C. 25
D. 10

48. Vest and jacket restraints are applied to the:

A. Wrists
B. Chest
C. Hand
D. Leg

49. Ms. Walsh has a restraint on her waist. You should check her she position of the restraint at least:

A. Every 3hours
B. Every 30 minutes
C. Every 2hours
D. Every 15 minutes

CIRCLE T IF THE STATEMENT IS TRUE AND F IF IT IS FALSE

50. Wrist restraints are used to prevent fall. T F

51. Restraints are used when the nurse thinks is needed. T F

52. Restraints are made of cloth or leather. T F

53. Some drugs are restraints. T F

54. Passive physical restraint does not totally restrict freedom of movement. T F

55. Restraints can increase confusion and agitation. T F

56. Restraints must be snug and firm, but not tight. T F

57. A vest restrains crosses at the back. T F

58. Tight restraints affect circulation and breathing. T F

59. Entrapment can occur between the bars of a bed rail. T F

60. Restraints require a doctor's order. T F

61. Every agency has policies and procedures for restraint use. T F

62. You can apply restraints when you think they are needed. T F

63. Older people are restrained more than younger people. T F

64. Restraints are used only once as a last resort to protect people from harming themselves or others. T F

65. The administration of vaccine to produce immunity against an infectious disease is called?

A. Vaccination
B. Vaccine
C. Immunity
D. Clean technique

66. The process of destroying all microbes is_______.

A. Germicide
B. Disinfection
C. Sterile
D. Sterilization

67. Hand washing is one way to prevent the spread of infectious agents' through_______.

A. Droplet
B. Airborne transmission
C. Direct contact
D. Food and water

68. Which of the following is not signs and symptoms of infection

A. Fever
B. High blood pressure
C. Nausea
D. Rash

69. Medical asepsis is the same as:

A. Normal flora
B. Surgical asepsis
C. Sterile technique
D. Clean technique

70. Protection against a certain disease is called:

A. Personal protective equipment
B. A germicide
C. Immunity
D. A vaccine

71. Between routine resident contacts, the CNA should wash his/her hands under running water for at least______

A. 10-15 seconds
B. 30 minutes
C. 5-6 minutes
D. 60 seconds

72. Standard precautions apply to;

A. Persons with infections
B. All doctors
C. All people
D. All residents

73. Microorganism grows best in_______.

A. Moist places
B. Hot environment
C. Dry places
D. High temperature

74. A wet or moist mask is ____________________.

A. Safe
B. Contaminated
C. Clean
D. Sterile

75. Masks are used for______________ precautions.

A. Standard
B. Isolation
C. Airborne
D. Contact

76. HIV and HBV are found in:

A. Blood
B. Intestine
C. Heart
D. Feces

77. HIV and hepatitis B are examples of a ________.

A. Rickettsia
B. Virus
C. Protozoa
D. Fungi

78. Hepatitis B is a ______ disease.

A. Kidney
B. Heart
C. Liver
D. Lungs

79. Asepsis means:

A. Being free of disease-producing microbes
B. Medical asepsis
C. Process of destroying pathogens
D. Protection against certain disease.

Circle T if the statement is true and F if it is false:

80. Gloves can be reuse. T F

81. Masks prevent spread of microbes from respiratory tract. T F

82. Specimens are transported to the laboratory in biohazard specimen bags. T F

83. All linen bags need a biohazard symbol. T F

84. Nosocomial infections are acquired during a stay in a health agency. T F

85. Unused Items in a person's room are used for another person. T F

86. A sterile package is contaminated when the expiration date has passed. T F

87. Isolation precaution prevents the spread of contagious diseases. T F

88. A pathogen can cause an infection. T F

89. Microbes need a reservoir to live and grow. T F

90. Using the body in an efficient and careful way is called:

A. Base of support
B. Posture
C. Body mechanics
D. Log rolling

91. These factors lead to back disorders except:

A. Turning whole body when changing direction of your movement.
B. Reaching while lifting.
C. Poor posture when sitting or standing.
D. Twisting while lifting.

92. Ergonomics is the science of________.

A. Balance
B. Body Alignment

C. Designing the job to fit the worker
D. Using body in an efficient way.

93. Which is a function of muscle to the body?

A. Movement of body parts.
B. Bearing of the body weight.
C. Protects the organs.
D. Pumps blood to the heart.

94. To change direction, a nurse aid should:

A. Move her body in section.
B. Mover her body slowly.
C. Twist from the waist.
D. Turn her whole body by moving her feet.

95. When repositioning a heavy client, the CNA should:

A. Move the client alone
B. Get a Co-Worker
C. Move the client hater
D. Get the family move the client.

96. Turning the person as a unit, in alignment with one motion is called:

A. Body Alignment
B. Ergonomics
C. Folding
D. Logrolling.

97. Stretchers are used to transport people who are________.

A. Disabled
B. Cannot sit up
C. Are mentally ill

D. Unsteady

98. A transfer belt is applied________.

A. Over clothing
B. Over bare skin
C. Over the breast
D. For the chest

99. As a CNA you should reposition a patient or resident at least every:

A. 3hours
B. 15 minute
C. Every 2 hours
D. 30 minutes

100. Lying on the abdomen with the head turned to one side is __________ position?

A. Lateral
B. Sims
C. Supine
D. Prone

101. In a semi-sitting position the head of the bed should be raised between_____ and ______.

A. 50degrees, 100degrees
B. 45degrees, 150 degrees
C. 100 degrees, 150 degrees
D. 45degrees, 90 degrees

102. In what position should unconscious patients be positioned when giving oral care?

A. Lateral position
B. Sims' position

C. Supine position
D. Prone position

103. To transfer a patient with a mechanical lift, at least_______________

A. One staff member is needed
B. Twelve staff members are needed
C. Two staff members are needed
D. Five staff members are needed

104. These statements are about positioning. Which one is incorrect?

A. Good position makes breathing easier and circulation is promoted.
B. It causes skin break down.
C. Proper positioning's helps prevent pressure ulcers and contractures
D. Regular position changes and good alignment promote comfort and well-being.

105. Which is not a guideline to safely position a person?

A. Use good body mechanics
B. As a co-worker to help you if needed
C. Twisting while moving the person
D. Explain the procedure to the person.

106. Transferring a client from a bed to a stretcher requires that the CNA use:

A. Proper body mechanics
B. Gait belt
C. Minimum of 5 workers
D. A Hoyer lift.

107. As a CNA when transferring a client from the bed to the wheelchair you should always_________

A. Place the paper or sheet under the person's feet
B. Lock the brakes on the wheelchair first.
C. Unlock the brakes on the wheel chair
D. Use mechanical lift.

108. Dangling a client's leg over the side of is done to:

A. To prevent pressure sores.
B. Give the client time to put on shoes
C. Make sure is able to sit up first.
D. Prevent orthostatic hypotension

109. Using a broad base of support means?

A. Keeping the feet comfortably apart
B. Keeping objects close to your body
C. Bending and reaching
D. keeping knees locked in place

110. When having a client to sit-up and dangle his legs before walking, the CNA should observe the following except:

A. Increased Respiration
B. Cheerfulness
C. Excessive sweating
D. Sudden paleness

111. Another name for transfer belt is ________.

A. Mechanical belt
B. Hoyer Lift
C. Gait belt
D. Waist belt

112. The rubbing of one surface against another is called:

A. Friction
B. Sharing
C. Logrolling
D. Posture

113. The left side lying position in which the upper leg is sharply flexed so it is not on the lower leg is called?

A. Supine position
B. Lateral Position
C. Prone position
D. Sims' position

114. Which of these can be used to lift and move the person in bed and reduce friction?

A. A spread
B. Drawsheet
C. A sheet
D. Blanket

115. The head of the bed is lowered, and the foot of the bed is raised, this position is called?

A. Fowler's position.
B. Semi-fowler's position.
C. Reverse trendelenburg's position.
D. Trendelenburg's position.

116. To prevent odor you should do the followings except:

A. Keeping laundry container open.
B. Changing soiled linen and clothing's promptly.
C. Checking incontinent person often.
D. Disposing of incontinence and ostomy products promptly.

117. People who are ill are sensitive to drafts, As a CNA to protect them you should do the followings except:

A. Make sure they wear the correct clothing.
B. Always leave them on drafty areas.
C. Cover them with blankets.
D. Offer lap blankets to those in chairs and wheelchairs.

118. OBRA requires that nursing centers should maintain a temperature range of:

A. 40 to 50 degrees Fahrenheit.
B. 100 to 150 degrees Fahrenheit.
C. 30 to 50 degrees Fahrenheit
D. 71 to 81 degrees Fahrenheit

119. Which people are the more sensitive to cold?

A. Older people
B. Younger people
C. Disabled people
D. Blind people

120. The patient and resident may find sounds dangerous, frightening or irritating and as a CNA to decrease noise you should______

A. Control your voice
B. Answer phones, signal lights and intercoms promptly
C. Handle equipment properly
D. All of the above

121. Good lightning is need for:

A. Low temperature
B. Blood circulation
C. Safety and comfort
D. Ventilation

122. Dull lightning can cause the following except:

A. Falls
B. Brain problem
C. Headaches
D. Eyestrain

123. People with poor vision needs________.

A. Dim light
B. Dull light
C. Bright light
D. No Light

124. Raising bed horizontally to give care reduces___________.

A. Bending and reaching
B. Twisting and jerking
C. Lifting and moving
D. Sitting and standing

125. Flatbed position is used after _________________.

A. Spinal cord injury
B. Surgery
C. Cervical traction
D. all of the above

126. When the head of the bed is raised to 3o degrees and the knee portion is raised 15 degrees; what position is this?

A. Fowler's
B. Semi-fowler
C. Trendelenburg's
D. Prone

127. Having the means to be completely free from the public view while in bed is___________>

A. In visual privacy
B. Curtain down privacy
C. Full visual privacy
D. Isolation

CIRCLE T IF IS TRUE AND F IF IT IS FALSE

128. OBRA requires that nursing center rooms be as homelike as possible. T F

129. People restricted to certain positions may need their bed locked. T F

130. Locking feature is useful for people with confusion or dementia. T F

131. Residents cannot bring some furniture and personal items from home. T F

132. Privacy curtains prevent others from seeing the person. T F

133. The overbed table and bedside stand should be within the person's reach. T F

134. Signal light should always be within the person's reach, in the room, bathroom and tub room. T F

135. A small sheet placed over the middle of bottom sheet is called:

A. Draw sheet
B. Fitted sheet
C. Top sheet
D. Mattress

136. A piece of linen that is placed beneath the client from shoulders to thigh is _______.

A. An underpad
B. Blanket
C. A drawsheet
D. A sheet

137. When making a bed, the CNA should place the soiled linen:

A. On the Resident's closet
B. In a laundry bag
C. On the floor
D. on the bedside table

138. CNA should always hold linens____________.

A. Close to their chest
B. On their heads
C. Towards their body
D. Away from their body and uniform.

139. Clean linens are placed on__________________.

A. Clean surface
B. On the floor
C. Dirty surface
D. Laundry containers

140. A surgical bed should be left in what position?

A. Lowest position
B. Semi-fowler's position
C. Highest Position
D. Fowler's position

141. When changing wet, damp, or soiled linens, you should always wear what?

A. Face shields
B. Gloves
C. Masks
D. Protective apparel

142. Which is not a rule for bed making?

A. Shaking linens before use
B. Use good body mechanics
C. Follow the rules of medical asepsis
D. Follow standard precautions and the blood borne pathogen standard.

143. The type of bed made for a person who is taken by the stretcher to treatment or therapy is called:

A. The closed bed
B. Open bed
C. Surgical bed
D. Occupied bed

144. Bed made for people who are out of their beds is called:

A. Occupied bed
B. Open bed
C. Close bed
D. Surgical bed

ANSWERS TO SECTION TWO

1. B
2. C
3. A
4. A
5. D
6. A
7. D
8. C
9. B
10. C
11. D
12. C
13. B
14. D
15. C
16. D
17. B
18. C
19. C
20. B
21. A
22. D
23. C
24. B
25. C
26. D
27. B
28. C
29. A
30. A
31. D
32. B
33. D

34. A
35. C
36. B
37. A
38. D
39. B
40. C
41. D
42. B
43. A
44. D
45. C
46. C
47. A
48. B
49. D
50. F
51. F
52. T
53. T
54. T
55. T
56. T
57. F
58. T
59. T
60. T
61. T
62. F
63. T
64. T
65. A
66. D
67. C
68. B
69. D
70. C

71. A
72. C
73. A
74. B
75. C
76. A
77. B
78. C
79. A
80. F
81. T
82. T
83. T
84. T
85. F
86. T
87. T
88. T
89. T
90. C
91. A
92. C
93. A
94. D
95. B
96. D
97. B
98. A
99. C
100. C
101. D
102. A
103. C
104. B
105. C
106. A
107. B

108. D
109. A
110. B
111. C
112. A
113. D
114. B
115. D
116. A
117. B
118. D
119. A
120. D
121. C
122. B
123. C
124. A
125. D
126. B
127. C
128. T
129. T
130. T
131. F
132. T
133. T
134. T
135. A
136. C
137. B
138. D
139. A
140. C
141. B
142. A
143. C
144. B

SECTION THREE

1. AM care is care that is given:

   A. After lunch
   B. Before lunch
   C. Before breakfast
   D. After breakfast

2. H.S is care that is given at what time?

   A. Before bed time
   B. After meal
   C. Before meal
   D. Upon awakening

3. As a CNA the first step in performing any procedure is to ________________.

   A. Provide privacy
   B. Explain the procedure
   C. Perform hand washing
   D. Introduce yourself by name and title

4. Before dressing a client the CNA should first:

   A. Report to charge nurse
   B. Provide privacy
   C. Choose the client's clothes
   D. Check the order

5. Gloves must be worn when:

   A. Feeding the a patient
   B. When combing a resident's hair
   C. Making bed
   D. Providing Peri-care

6. Afternoon care involves the following except:

   A. Assisting with elimination
   B. Cleaning incontinent people
   C. Brushing client's teeth
   D. Changing wet or soiled linens and garments.

7. The medical abbreviation for 'before the meal' is____________.

   A. qid
   B. a.c
   C. p.c
   D. bid

8. It is important to always practice standard precaution when____________.

   A. Dressing a patient
   B. Providing oral hygiene
   C. Ambulating a patient
   D. Feeding a patient

9. The safe water temperature for complete bed bath is_________________.

   A. 50° F
   B. 80° F
   C. 110° F
   D. 150° F

10. The purpose of perinea care is to

   A. Prevent skin breakdown
   B. Prevent infection

C. Prevent itching, burning and body odor
D. All of the above

CIRCLE T IF THE STATEMENT IS TRUE AND F IF IT IS FALSE

11. Odors and discomfort occurs if perinea areas are not clean. T F

12. Back massages last 3 to 5 minutes. T F

13. Lotion reduces friction during massage. T F

14. Fowler's position is best for a massage. T F

15. Back massage relaxes muscles and stimulates circulation. T F

16. The normal water temperature for perinea care is 150°F. T F

17. Perineal care is also done whenever the area is soiled with urine and feces. T F

18. Perineal area is delicate and easily injured. T F

19. Weak people can be left alone in the shower if they are sitting down. T F

20. Flossing removes plaque and tartar from the teeth. T F

21. Perineal care helps prevent infection and body odor. T F

22. Excessive body hair in women and children is called:

A. Hirsutism
B. Alopecia
C. Pediculosis

D. Dandruff

23. Brushing and combing hair are part of______________ care.

A. Afternoon care
B. Night care
C. Morning care
D. Midnight care

24. As a CNA when giving hair care to a client you should place the towel:

A. On the client's leg
B. At her/his back
C. On the stomach
D. Across the shoulder

25. The CNA should record and report the following observation:

A. Presence of lice
B. Length of hair
C. Flaking
D. All of the above

26. Nail and foot care prevents the following except:

A. Infection
B. Injury
C. Fall
D. Odors

27. The first rule for changing client's gown and clothing is:

A. Provide privacy
B. Encourage the person to do as much as possible
C. Let the person choose what to wear

D. Raising the bed for body mechanics

28. When changing clothing, you need the following information from the nurse and care plan except:

A. How much help the person needs.
B. If the person needs to wear certain garments.
C. What observations to report and record.
D. How to position the person.

29. What observation do you need to report and record when giving nail and foot care?

A. The shape of the nails.
B. Any abnormalities.
C. Any complaints by the person
D. All of the above.

30. When giving foot care you should soak the client feet for___________ minutes.

A. 15 to 20 minutes
B. 10 to 20 minutes
C. 15 to 30 minutes
D. 5 to 10 minutes

31. The following are needed when giving nail care except:

A. Orange stick
B. Hand towel
C. Kidney basin
D. Electric shavers

CIRCLE T IF THE STATEMENT IS TRUE AND F IF IT IS FALSE.

32. Razor blades are used to shave people who take anticoagulant drugs. T F

33. Feet are not easily infected and injured. T F

34. Brushing increases blood flow to one's scalp. T F

35. Nails are easier to trim after soaking or bathing. T F

36. Foot injuries are very serious for older people and those with circulatory disorders. T F

37. The loss of bladder control is called:

A. Urinary urgency
B. Urge incontinence
C. Urinary Incontinence
D. Stress incontinence

38. Another name for voiding is____________.

A. Urination
B. Dysuria
C. Vomiting
D. Nocturia

39. These substances increases urine production except:

A. Coffee
B. Cereals
C. Tea
D. Alcohol

40. Factors Affecting urine production are:

A. Age
B. Dietary salt
C. Body temperature
D. All of the above

41. Which of these is not causes of urinary frequency?

A. Trauma
B. Bladder infection
C. Pressure on the bladder
D. Excess fluid intake

42. Causes of hematuria include the followings except:

A. Kidney disease
B. Shock
C. Urinary tract infection
D. Trauma

43. A tube used to drain or inject fluid through a body opening is called:

A. Foley catheter
B. Catherization
C. A catheter
D. Micturition

44. A urinary catheter drains________.

A. Intestine
B. Blood
C. Feces
D. Urine

45. Healthy adult produces about_______ ml (millimeters) of urine a day.

A. 1200
B. 1500

C. 3000
D. 500

46. You should not apply a condom catheter if the penis is________________.

A. Long
B. Red
C. Firm
D. Thick

47. The excessive formation of gases in the stomach and intestine is called:

A. Flatus
B. Fecal impaction
C. Feces
D. Flatulence

48. One of these is not a cause of fecal incontinence.

A. Intestinal diseases
B. Constipation
C. Irritable bowel syndrome
D. Nervous system diseases

49. Doctors order Enemas for the following reason except:

A. To remove feces
B. To relieve constipation
C. To increase blood circulation
D. To clean the bowel off feces before certain surgeries and diagnostic procedures.

50. Enema tube is usually inserted___ to ____ inches in adults.

A. 3 to 4

B. 5 to 10
C. 10 to 15
D. 2 to 3

51. In what position should a client positioned when giving Enema

A. Prone position
B. Fowler's position
C. Supine position
D. Lateral position

52. Which statement about the oil-retention Enema is incorrect?

A. It relieves constipation and fecal impaction.
B. Retaining oil hardening feces.
C. It lets feces pass with ease.
D. The oil is retained for 30 to 60 minutes

53. The purpose of a rectal tube is to:

A. To gain control of bowel movement.
B. To build up feces in the rectum.
C. Relieve flatulence and intestinal distention
D. To develop a regular pattern of elimination

54. Surgically Created Opening between the colon and abdominal wall is called:

A. Colostomy
B. An ostomy
C. Ileostomy
D. Peristalsis

55. Causes of diarrhea include the following except:

A. Infections
B. Irritating food
C. Shock
D. Microbes in food and water.

56. Which one is not signs and symptoms of dehydration?

A. Flushed skin
B. Soft Skin
C. Coated tongue
D. Oliguria

57. The backward flow of food from the stomach into the mouth is:

A. Anorexia
B. Regurgitation
C. Enteral nutrition
D. Dehydration

58. A tube inserted through a surgically created opening into the stomach is called:

A. Jejunostomy tube
B. Nasointestinal tube
C. Gastrostomy tube
D. Nasogastric tube

59. The swelling of body tissues with is __________.

A. Enema
B. Edema
C. Dehydration
D. Gauage

60. The amount of energy produced when the body burns food is called:

A. A Calorie
B. A nutrient
C. Nutrition
D. Dietary

61. Poor eating and poor diet habits causes the following:

A. Chronic illness to become worse
B. Healing problems
C. Increase the risk for acute and chronic diseases
D. All of the above

62. Involuntary muscle contractions called _________ moves the food down the esophagus into the stomach.

A. Peristalsis
B. Pancreas movement
C. Dysphagia
D. Anus

63. One gram of fat produces ______ calories.

A. 6
B. 4
C. 9
D. 8

64. Which is the function of vitamin D?

A. Formation of red blood cell.
B. Absorption and metabolism of calcium and phosphorus.
C. Blood clotting

D. Muscle function

65. All are functions of vitamin C except (ascorbic acid) except:

A. Nervous system function.
B. Formation of substances that hold tissues together.
C. Prevention of bleeding
D. Wound healing

66. Sources of vitamin B_2 include the following except:

A. Milk
B. Liver
C. Green leafy vegetables
D. Pork

67. Which mineral allows red blood cells to carry oxygen?

A. Potassium
B. Iron
C. Iodine
D. Calcium

68. Which statement about carbohydrates is false?

A. It provides energy and fiber for bowel movement.
B. They are only found in breads.
C. Carbohydrates breakdown into sugar during digestion.
D. It provides the bulky part of chime for elimination.

69. Factors affecting nutrition and eating habits are:

A. Age
B. Culture
C. Finances
D. All of the above

70. Causes of anorexia involve the followings except:

A. Rash
B. Anxiety
C. Pain
D. Depression

71. Diabetes meal planning is for people with_________.

A. Mental problem
B. Dementia
C. Diabetes mellitus
D. HIV

72. Diabetes is a chronic disease from lack of _________________________________.

A. Vitamins
B. Water
C. Insulin
D. Sugar

73. If fluid intake exceeds fluid output, body tissues swell with water. This is called what?

A. Edema
B. Dehydration
C. Fluid Balance
D. Flow rate

74. A measuring container for fluid is called:

A. Gauage
B. Cylinder
C. Cone
D. Graduate

75. A graduate is used to measure the following except:

A. Left over fluids
B. Feces
C. Urine
D. Vomitus

76. Intravenous (IV) therapy means____________.

A. Use of foods and fluids by the body.
B. Amount of fluid taking in.
C. Fluids Guide pyramid
D. Giving fluids through a needle or catheter inserted into a vein.

77. The following norm requirements under OBRA promotes quality of life and comfort, rest and sleep, except:

A. Clean and orderly room
B. Room with more than 4 people
C. Room temperature between 71° F and 81°F
D. Adequate ventilation and room humidity

78. Which of the following is not a kind of pain?

A. Acute pain
B. Chronic pain
C. Insomnia pain
D. Radiating pain

79. Pain from a heart attack is often felt in the following areas except:

A. Left chest
B. Right shoulder
C. Left Arm
D. Left shoulder

80. Pain felt at the site of tissue damage and is nearby is ________________.

A. Radiating pain
B. Chronic pain
C. Phantom pain
D. Acute pain

81. Acute pain last for a short time and is usually less than _______ months.

A. Two
B. Ten
C. Six
D. Eight

82. Mr. Johnson was given a drug for pain, to protect him from injury. You should do the following except:

A. Raise the bed in the high position
B. Provide help if he needs to get up
C. Raise bed rails as directed
D. Check on him every ten to fifteen minutes

83. Which words are not used to describe pain?

A. Cramping
B. Standing
C. Burning
D. Gnawing

84. Factors affecting reactions to pain include______________________.

A. Past experience

B. Anxiety
C. Age
D. All of the above

85. Which one is a sign and symptom of pain?

A. Low blood pressure
B. Dry skin
C. Nausea
D. Cold

85. Relaxation means ___________________.

A. To be calm, at ease and relaxed
B. To be free from mental and physical stress
C. A state of unconsciousness
D. A state of well-being.

87. MR. Johnson has a blood transfusion going on. For the first one hour, he should be checked at least every:

A. 25 minutes
B. 5 minutes
C. 15 minutes
D. 30 minutes

88. Which one is not nursing measure to promote comfort and relieve pain?

A. Applying hot applications
B. Assisting with elimination needs
C. Keeping bed linens tight and wrinkle free
D. Positioning the person in good alignment

89. Circadian rhythm is a daily rhythm based on a __________ hour cycle.

A. 6

B. 10
C. 12
D. 24

90. The average sleep requirements for newborns (birth to 4 weeks) per day is:

A. 11 to 12 hours per day
B. 14 to 18 hours per day
C. 12 to 14 hours per day
D. 10 to 11 hours per day

91. A chronic condition in which the person cannot sleep or stay asleep all night is called___________.

A. Distraction
B. REM Sleep
C. Insomnia
D. Discomfort

92. Who orders bed rest?

A. CNA
B. Respiratory Therapist
C. Doctor
D. Occupational Therapist.

93. Bed rest is ordered for the following reasons except:

A. Reduce pain
B. Promote blood circulation
C. Encourage rest
D. Regain rest

94. Lack of joint mobility caused by abnormal shortening of muscle is ___________________.

A. Contracture
B. Atrophy

C. Dislocation
D. Syncope

95. Orthostatic hypotension means:

A. Excessive straightening of a body part
B. Brief Loss of consciousness
C. Abnormal high blood pressure
D. Abnormally low blood pressure when the person suddenly stands up.

96. Medical abbreviation for "range of motion" is:

A. RFM
B. ROM
C. RUQ
D. RPM

97. Another name for orthostatic hypotension is:

A. Blood Hypotension
B. Contractual hypotension
C. Postural hypotension
D. Syncope

98. Trochanter rolls helps to ______________.

A. Keep the hips abducted
B. Prevent contractures of thumbs, fingers and wrist.
C. Keep the weight of top linen off the feet and toes
D. The hips and legs from turning outward.

99. A trapeze is used for:

A. Exercises to strengthen arm muscles
B. Bending the foot down at the ankle.
C. Rotation of joint

D. Straightening of a body part

100. Range of motion exercise are usually done at least ____________ times a day.

A. 5
B. 2
C. 3
D. 6

101. CNA should record and report the following observations to the charge nurse when performing range of motion exercise to clients:

A. Complaints of pain or signs of stiffness or spasm
B. The time the exercise was performed
C. The joint exercised
D. All of the above

CIRCLE T IF THE STATEMENT IS TRUE AND F IF IT IS FALSE

102. Passive range of motion exercise is done by the person. T F

103. Trapeze is also used to move-up and turn bed. T F

104. Adduction is moving a body part away from the midline of the body. T F

105. Exercise Helps prevents contractures, muscle atrophy. T F

106. Canes provide balance and support. T F

107. Four-point canes give more support than single-tip canes. T F

108. A cuff and measuring device used to measure blood pressure is:

A. Sphygmomanometer
B. Stethoscope
C. Adjustable value
D. Manometer

109. The normal pulse rate for adult is __________.

A. 80-190 per minute
B. 80-160 per minute
C. 70-110 per minute
D. 60-100 per minute

110. Which pulse rate is taking during CPR and other emergencies?

A. Femoral
B. Carotid
C. Popliteal
D. Brachial

111. Most often used pulse which is easy to reach and find is:

A. Carotid
B. Apical
C. Radial
D. Pedal

112. As a CNA which of the following set of vital signs should you report to the charge nurse immediately?

A. T-99.6, P-82, R-16, BP-130/70
B. T-98.6, P-65, R-18, BP-120/60
C. T-97.6, P-81, R-20, BP-110/60
D. T-105.5, P-100, R-40, BP-180/100

113. The pulse located in the neck is called:

A. Carotid
B. Temporal
C. Brachial
D. Femoral

114. Most accurate method of measuring body temperature is ____________________.

A. Axial
B. Oral
C. Rectal
D. Tympanic

115. The order "vital signs T.I.D" means to record vital signs:

A. Every other day
B. Three times a day
C. Twice a day
D. Four times a day

116. Which of these is a factor that does not increase pulse rate?

A. Fear
B. Anxiety
C. Pain
D. Sleep

117. Rectal temperatures are not taken if the person has the following except:

A. Diabetes
B. Diarrhea
C. Rectal disorder or injury

D. Confusion or is agitated

118. The amount of force needed to pump blood out of the heart into the arterial circulation is:

A. Diastolic pressure
B. Body temperature
C. Systolic pressure
D. Blood pressure

119. CNA must use a stethoscope to determine the ________________.

A. Pedal pulse rate
B. Apical pulse rate
C. Femoral pulse rate
D. Brachial pulse rate

CIRCLE T IF THE STATEMENT IS TRUE AND F IF IT IS FALSE.

120. Admission process starts at the admitting office. T F

121. Height and weight are measured on admission. T F

122. Robe and slippers are worn when the person is measured. T F

123. Transfer usually relates to change in condition. T F

124. CNA can plan a client discharge. T F

125. If a person complains of pain, you should report it immediately. T F

126. Chair and lift scales are used for people who cannot stand. T F

127. A digital scale should read at zero. T F

128. To measure weight gain or loss, the person should be weighed daily, weekly or monthly. T F

129. Before breakfast is the best time to weigh a person. T F

130. Food and fluids add weight. T F

131. Identifying information is obtained when the person arrives in the nursing unit. T F

132. You can use admission records to find the person's name. T F

133. During admission procedure you will orient the person about the room, the nursing unit and the agency. T F

134. Admission to a nursing center or hospital causes anxiety and fear in patients. T F

135. A lighted instrument used to examine the external ear and the eardrum is called:

A. Ophthalmoscope
B. Telescope
C. Oscilloscope
D. Manometer

136. Which Of these is used to examine the inside of the nose?

A. Laryngeal mirror
B. Nasal speculum
C. Ophthalmoscope
D. Oscilloscope

137. Dorsal recumbent position is used to examine the following except:

A. Abdomen
B. Breasts
C. Chest
D. Spinal cord

138. The lithotomy position is used to examine what?

A. Vagina
B. Breast
C. Rectum
D. Heart

139. An Instrument used to open the Vagina so it and cervix can be examine is called:

A. Nasal speculum
B. Percussion Hammer
C. Vaginal speculum
D. Turning fork.

ANSWERS FOR SECTION THREE

1. C
2. A
3. C
4. B
5. D
6. C
7. B
8. B
9. C
10. D
11. T
12. T
13. T
14. F
15. T
16. F
17. T
18. T
19. F
20. T
21. T
22. A
23. C
24. D
25. D
26. C
27. A
28. D
29. D
30. A
31. D
32. F
33. T
34. T
35. T
36. T

37. C
38. A
39. B
40. D
41. A
42. B
43. C
44. D
45. B
46. B
47. D
48. B
49. C
50. A
51. D
52. B
53. C
54. A
55. C
56. B
57. B
58. C
59. B
60. A
61. D
62. A
63. C
64. B
65. A
66. D
67. B
68. B
69. D
70. A
71. C
72. C
73. A

74. D
75. B
76. D
77. B
78. C
79. B
80. A
81. C
82. A
83. B
84. D
85. C
86. B
87. C
88. A
89. D
90. B
91. C
92. C
93. B
94. A
95. D
96. B
97. C
98. D
99. A
100. B
101. D
102. F
103. T
104. F
105. T
106. T
107. T
108. A
109. D
110. B

111. C
112. D
113. A
114. C
115. B
116. D
117. A
118. C
119. B
120. T
121. T
122. F
123. T
124. F
125. T
126. T
127. T
128. T
129. T
130. T
131. F
132. T
133. T
134. T
135. C
136. B
137. D
138. A
139. C